WARRIOR'S CAREER

By the same author

Poems
The Railings
The Lions' Mouths
Sandgrains on a Tray

For children
Brownjohn's Beasts
To Clear the River *(as John Berrington)*

WARRIOR'S CAREER

POEMS BY ALAN BROWNJOHN

PR
6052
R62
W3

MACMILLAN

© Alan Brownjohn 1972

All rights reserved. No part of this publication
may be reproduced or transmitted, in any form or
by any means, without permission

SBN boards: 333 13614 4
SBN paper: 333 13615 2

First published 1972 by
MACMILLAN LONDON LTD
London and Basingstoke
Associated companies in New York Toronto
Dublin Melbourne Johannesburg & Madras

Printed in Great Britain by
ALAN POOLEY PRINTING LTD.

L.C.

Acknowledgements are due to the editors of the following, in which various of these poems first appeared: *Ambit, Antaeus* (U.S.A.), *Aquarius,* the Dial-a-Poem service of the Greater London Arts Association, *Galaxy* (Oxford University Press), *The Listener, New Statesman, The Occasional Windhover, Poetry and Audience, The Poetry Review, Quarry* (Canada), Sceptre Press Poets, Sycamore Poets, *The Times Literary Supplement, Wave,* and the BBC Radio Three programme *Poetry Now.*

CONTENTS

Ode to Melancholy	1
The Packet	3
Connection	4
Woman Reading Aloud	5
White Night	8
Weathers	9
Projection	10
Ballad of Scarlet and Black	12
A Day by Indirections	14
Elizabeth Pender's Dream of Friendship	16
Sadly on Barstools	19
Formosavej	20
Crabwise	21
Epithalamium	23
In a Convent Garden	24
Calypso for Sir Bedivere	26
Engagements in Armour	31
Told by a Monk	32
Pastoral	36
Transformation Scene	38
Palindrome	41
Weeping Doll	42
Ode to Centre Point	44
Frateretto Calling	48
A Politician	50
Clerk	51
Leo	52
Synopsis	53
Notes on Some of the Poems	55

ODE TO MELANCHOLY

for Martin Bell

I have made England
almost
unusable with associations. Every

beach, square, terrace or
shattered chancel has its
touchy girl, saying

'Don't go back *there*.'
                       So
on Bank Holiday I walk
home, home in the sun. Little

cats jump their heads into
my hand, but I can't talk
to *people*. Closing

my door, it's eight hours
playing and refining the
games of melancholia :

cushions, records,
crumbling sugar-heaps,
self-love. O gentle, helpful

melancholy, give me
one good doodle on a
white page for

all my afternoon's journey;
rescind time's
importance for me so I don't

care how the days of the week are
seven, the days of the month are
seven plus twenty-one; and

feed me black coffee, black
cigarettes, black socks
(toujours

la delicatesse!) — that I can
wait so happily for
darkness to require

all those curtains to be pulled.

THE PACKET

In the room,
In the woman's hand as she turns
Is the packet of salt.

On the packet is a picture of a
Woman turning,
With a packet in her hand.

When the woman in the room com-
Pletes her turning, she
Puts the packet down and leaves.

On the packet in the picture
Is: a picture of a woman
Turning, with a packet in her hand.

On this packet is a picture: of a woman,
Turning, with a packet in her hand.
On this packet is no picture

 — It is a tiny blank.
       And now the man waits,
And waits: two-thirty, seven-thirty,
Twelve.

At twelve he lays the packet on its side
And draws, in the last packet in the last
Picture, a tiny woman turning.

And then he locks the door,
And switches off the bedside lamp,
And among the grains of salt he goes to sleep.

CONNECTION

The first take was an offer in eagerness,
With every white finger so quickly threading,
Those hands went on as if they didn't think.

But they thought for the second take; which was
A slow agreed advancing, and a
Watching with eyes to see what eyes would tell.

The third take was from longer forethought, becoming
A turmoil and grating of little, decorated
Bones; neither hand wanted it.
                              In fact,

The fourth take might never have been at all,
Except . . . . some kind of separateness travelled
The arm to the shoulder, the shoulder to the brain

And there it spoke: to separate, such hands
Needed to have been joined
                            and been confused

— Once more those fingers did as they were used.

WOMAN READING ALOUD

A tree looked at won't
ever react,
      because it
must go on only with
its own sufficient life.
      But a
person, a woman say, isn't
particularly
      like that.
Contemplating people
modifies them a little.
      I'd be
embarrassed,
      or some worse thing,
to be regarded, if
I were beautiful.
      Too
much of it could begin
to work
changes
      — any
-thing beautiful looked at
starts to be quite
      conscious,
wants to vary away from itself,
can't keep the first
one
      position you first
admired it in,
      desires
alterations of treatment,
      you

have to keep
up with it (your
 own fault).
For these reasons, I'd
think it was still
 all right
to make statues of stone or bronze quite
exactly: exactly the same as
their subjects,
 or
to trace out the mild
breathings of particular lips
with line and word and colon
as nearly as lips could wish,
as if to say:
 look,
only here, yes, only
here.
 This
used to be done just
against the hatreds of time,
 but
we could do it, still, to
love the constructed thing instead,
while
the beauty was let go
forward, not checked
 not self
- conscious, and a little
less changed.
 Which
is not to sanction flattery.
After all, it would be
 wonder
-ful if the
 stone or bronze were so
near the unquestionable truth that

it felt it could
really
        step
        down,
and actually breathe,
        in beautiful,
living ordinariness, lawful
as eating.
        Or if
there were suddenly those
words I had written,
        on that
page accidentally left on a bare table,
and that
was
their sound,
        spoken
(as they met me, crossing
a room when not
expected, towards her
        slim
shoulders which so
hate flattery)
        words
so truthful and agreed
        they
had themselves become the mild
breathings of
        the particular
lips.

WHITE NIGHT

I did not dream it, no I *was*
A t.v. screen left on shining, and
Insensately vibrating, and
Blank, in a shop at night: like a
Flat yet restless pool.

I could picture nothing; but
I was alive and was shivering and
Wanting to hold more and think more
Than grey, sudden flecks and bleak dots
Momently repeating.

O nice insomnia, fastidiously
Beckoning the abrasive dawn, and tuning
The mind to that first, drab
Water-table where, out of such cold depths,
      came
Monsters on which the hurtful body rode.

WEATHERS

The man rummages the intonations of her voice.
He wonders if she will proffer the cigarette.
The filament of the fire clicks once.

She rises with the cigarettes pointing.
She goes to the second woman first, who refuses.
The lights flicker as if his eye had blinked.

She goes to the second man second:
He accepts. She goes back poising her own cigarette.
The draught teems at the stopped-up door.

From her chair she offers now the first man
A cigarette. He takes it quickly, and nods.
A spray of rain patters the reflecting glass.

It is not that they speak. The first man leans
Rapidly to the matches on the table, strikes one.
The clouds of the night outside shift among themselves.

He lights the woman's cigarette, the second man's,
And then his own; relapses eagerly to his chair.
A pitiable vain wind hawks the marshes in darkness.

PROJECTION

And that midnight raced across
Down the sand, James Carra first. And
Though the air drenched his eyes,
Suddenly he saw the thing, the figure, his
Own shadow running terribly forwards onto

Him, out of the water; because all these four
People were running straight down the
Headlight path in the dark to the shallow
Sea, and had met their ghosts rearing
Up from the tide-edge. Where

The water stood them, the four stood
In quiet and disquiet, trying to trace
The invisible lip of the retrenching
Tide. The sea was unseizably dark.
This distance, the car lights couldn't

Choose out one wave-crest; but then the water
Was blankly calm where the four
Stopped, and couldn't speak, before
Their huge grey shapes hovering
And diffusing upon the Atlantic. Such

Ghosts they were content to own,
Knowing their nature, the un-
Measurable powerlessness of shadows. And when
They turned back up their glaring track
Those vast greynesses comfortingly

Dwindled again (slowly, because they walked)
Dwindled into the sea again, that did
Nothing. Only James Carra, walking,
Thought more than this, as he measured out the
Dark sand and caught at his disrupted breath

— As he knew she would catch, who
Lay across the water in the
Drowning sheets, checking her
Breath for a lover on whom no
Writs or shadows he could cast could run.

BALLAD OF SCARLET AND BLACK

Waking at her lover's knocking, or
So she thought, she crossed, running,
A carpet twenty yards wide
To the curtains at the window, scarlet-
And-black,
And drew them.

Or so she thought.
                Because
Behind the first curtains were
More curtains, and behind
The second were third,
And behind the third were fourth, none
Of them opening into daylight and onto
Her lover's face waiting at her door,
But onto only
Scarlet-and-black and then
Scarlet-and-black and then
Scarlet-and-black.

But several seconds later truly waking,
She drew
The curtains which were not in her dream,
And were one foot from her bed,
And were scarlet-and-black
And let straight daylight immediately in.

So now she combed, at her mirror, with
Fingers over open eyes, a parting in her hair,
              counting
Which day of daylight this was, and counting
The years of her life again.

And when her lover called, she
Went across town with him talking of her dream
              and what it meant,
Talking of their parting, and joining, and their
              endless counting of time,
And she was trying, trying to uncover
His daylight face.

Up the stairs to his room,
Their blood was the blood of veins returning
              to the heart,
Returning as if with ritual nostalgia
              to the heart,
Between scarlet and black.

There, pulling the black,
Lying under the scarlet, curtains, unhooked
              from the wall,
They made again the love of years,
With his face in darkness;
And then, with fingers across closed eyes
She sorted apart her hair
And slept until the next daylight arrived
              to be counted.

A DAY BY INDIRECTIONS

The lovers in the dark quarrel and deny one
    another up the sides of a pyramid they
Are building of hate and sleep. But they meet
    at five in one point in one
Cry over their covered store of uncontradictable
    gold.

The man runs the wrong corridor at ten, finds the
    expected upward staircase
Rattling to meet him downwards, turns a corner and
    loses his ticket for the barrier
But has his friend's number when he breathes back
    sense into himself in the corner seat.

The friend sits at his table at one, recalls
    an eccentric kindness and
Tells him the story looking at his wife all
    the time. But it
Comes to the man through that smile, though it is
    not into his own eyes at all.

The stranger asks a long question at four,
    stretches out to the end
Blindly through gauzes of circumlocution,
    but walks out at last
To the daylight of a place where something can
    be answered.

At seven the foreground goes with the man in the
 returning train, but the middle
Distance flees back in a sliding wedge of sheep and
 hedges; but the horizon
Always keeps up, and keeps his valuable sun in
 a weird and moving balance.

ELIZABETH PENDER'S DREAM OF FRIENDSHIP

When all these men and
women came, in
the sunlight, to that
        tower they
found it
was embedded
in the earth. And
to get inside, you
crossed over this
iron bridge, to meet
spiralling
        downward
steps;
which they did,
and proceeded down
-stairs to a room
with only a
white
telephone in it and one
window looking out at hills
barely holding back the sea.
And when the
telephone immediately
        rang,
a voice told them
don't
go, whatever
else you do, out
by the middle stair
-case door if the
        horse
is standing in the field with

tresses of blood-wet
silk at its mouth.
How then to
        get away,
all these lovers and friends,
because when
they
        opened that door,
they saw, in blank fright,
the enormous horse
waiting
        and looking
and waiting,
and they must not, could
not go out. Still,
at the top of the spiral of
steps, it was a
hundred fears worse:
a darkening
field of
broken
inscribed
        graves, which moved
and edged to
-wards them,
and utterly white
funerary
        statues,
embracing.
At that top door, they
held one
another tightly, but
        who,
when they looked,
exactly
        who
were their friends?

Because one by
one, everyone
      not
thoroughly true to her,
or to himself,
or to herself,
was irrevocably
      dissolving,
and it was starting to
be, very suddenly,
      night.
It was so
      black now, they
couldn't even make out
which of each other's
faces
were still
truly
      there,
in which fear,
she, and they, tried
hard (it was so
hard now) to breathe, and tried
to speak, and tried to
think how possible in any
-thing like this, any
-thing like
      dawn
actually

was.

SADLY ON BARSTOOLS

Sadly on barstools, in a city which doesn't speak
English with their accents, two have come together
Of whom one is asking the other advice, very frankly,
About a third — to whom neither is connected
By blood, or sexual ravin: just anxious friends,
And wanting to save Amanda's and William's marriage
                              because
They prefer it that way.

The drinks, the bar, the barman, the fast bar clock
Are spun away to nothing among a cat's cradle
Of lovely information and speculation: who
Should, for whose future good, intervene
With whom, and if possible when,
And as between Friday in Greenwich or Sunday in
                              Islington,
It isn't decided yet.

Common citizens unlike them, and more usual in this place,
Are flocking round,
With ordinary drinks that have not seriously, ever,
Strained the cellars of the Bull. The television,
Shoved on the shelf above the forgotten picture
Of part of the local docks in 1910, is showing
A retrospective tribute to Michael Miles.

FORMOSAVEJ

The tramway ran out along into the night,
Its rails were wet from the rain and the tramway continu
It met houses, it met shops, it met parks, it met cafés,
It met dogs.

And in the shining of
The light of the lamps in the rain on its tracks
It went steadily on with its own quiet, metal
Wilfulness all the time.

On it, the brittle
Narrow, bright, single-decker trams rang and
Rattled: busy and green-grey frameworks
Of glitter and rightness.

At the many turns
In the wide streets and the by-streets their
Brakes drew in breath and groaned, at
Jolts and bumps on the track all the dainty
Lights went off and came on again.

Overhead, through all this,
The wires droned and thudded and crackled
And at sudden halts all the empty red-leather
Seats reversed themselves.

When the terminus came,
It was a splendid aggregation of trams on
The circle of tracks at the end of the route,
A stupefying, fascinating, memorable
    Clatter of numbers

And lights and signs and conductors and drivers
And cheerful spitting sparks at the knots
In the overhead wires. Readers, you would have
    Enjoyed this as much as I did.

CRABWISE

        Sea-crabs live in
        And near the sea,
        Land-crabs go back
        Occasionally.

After these many months the old crab was out of the water,
And into the full, blank air and wanting the sun.

        A crab has a very strange
        Sideways walk
        And eyes placed on
        A retracting stalk.

Wide sheets of wet light covered the level beach
As he came fumbling and peering over the gnarled sand.

        Two kinds of bodies
        For crabs there are:
        The oval and
        The triangular.

His ten legs carried his squat bulk grave-
ly and slowly like a burden altogether too sad to keep long,

        A little crab only
        Really begins
        To be adult when he's
        Cast five skins.

This was his last stroll of years out of the bitter flow and
Hard swirl of the winter water, dragging from pool to clear pool.

> A crab's feet are not
> All the same, because
> Some are for walking
> And some have jaws.

His old mouths muttered on the windy silence as he walked.
In his funny clumsiness and misery he was man-like.

EPITHALAMIUM

Two by two this Saturday you little animals
Step with your decoration of hymns and flowers in-
To your waiting compounds; taking your place among all
The ancient objects of living, those graceless
Gifts that will stick for years, like burrs out of reach;
There being, always:
                      Blankets to cover you,
Curtains to curtain you, clocks that will thread your
Disquieted sleeps with duty, and sets of knives.
In all South London a misted orange heaven
Haloes the nurtured hair and suits of smiles.

But in some other uncertain sunlight, of a bad dream,
Such things may rise like some
Sortilegious army, shuddering the compounds,
Greedy to seize their own power and
Wailing in rancour: Can you depart us,
Dismiss us, divide us? — And will need to be
Put down somehow in baskets and sacks
And cases and bags and pockets and
Arranged elsewhere, in a place where they can always be
      seen,
With snarls that stay on their faces until you die.

IN A CONVENT GARDEN

In the convent vegetable garden the nuns
Have erected a scarecrow in front of the runner beans,
And it has an old wimple on its head.

In the spring the beans will climb, will climb
But the crows are coming:
The wimple will chase them away.

In the convent vegetable garden the nuns
Have erected a scarecrow alongside the cauliflowers,
And it has an old wimple on its head.

In the spring the cauliflowers will rise, will rise
But the daws are deadly:
The wimple will drive them away.

In the convent vegetable garden the nuns
Have erected a scarecrow behind the marrow plants,
And it has an old wimple on its head.

In the spring the marrows will expand will expand
But the tits are terrible:
The wimple will turn them away.

In the summer the marrows will fructify completely,
And will be scrubbed under rubber-nozzled taps and peeled
And sliced and cored and mutton shoved inside

And the scarecrow will be taken apart
And at the long tables in the cool refectory
The Mother Superior and the nuns and the novice nuns
        and the symbolists will sit and stuff
                themselves for a considerable
                      length of time.

CALYPSO FOR SIR BEDIVERE

But it was not only a sword to me,
It was a symbol, like, of virility.

King Arthur said, 'Take the sword away,
Throw it back into that lake today.'

> *Now King Arthur was a*
> *Wise old king,*
> *But why should he under*
> *-Stand everything?*

So I went down as a loyal knight should
And looked at the lake in an uneasy mood,

And was shaping to throw the sword in the water
When suddenly a very subliminal thought o-

Curred to me: 'Whoever *wants* to lose
A trusty weapon that is still some use,

'A rational man would want to retain
His faithful tool and use it again,

> *King Arthur may be a*
> *Wise old king,*
> *But is he tuned in to*
> *Everything?'*

So with this sensible reasoning,
I stashed the sword and went back to the king,

And to change the subject I stood and lied
About the marvellous, marvellous countryside.

But the king said, 'I can quite well see
There are one or two things you are not telling me,

'Go back and throw that sword in the lake,
Tell me what you see, make no mistake.'

> *King Arthur was a*
> *Wise old king,*
> *But why should he have to guess*
> *Everything?*

Well, a second time I went down to the edge
And took out the sword to fulfil my pledge,

And cast it, for the king, out into that mere,
When suddenly I thought, 'No, I *can't* stand here

And fling this thing into that dirty pool,
It's a work of art, and valuable:

> *King Arthur may be a*
> *Wise old king,*
> *But does he know the cost of*
> *Everything?'*

So another time I went back up along
And told the king how I'd stood there, long

Time gazing at the lovely scenery
 — But still he was not believing me.

He said, 'Go back down and take that blade
And throw it in the water just like I said'.

Then I thought:

With the king being terribly stern to me,
Can I prick against the kicks of authority?

So a third time, then, I went down to the brink
And looked at the water, as black as ink,

And picked up the sword (what else could I do?)
And with one strong, well-meaning lunge I threw

It right out *there*.
 . . . . There was a clatter and I saw it drop
On the flat of its blade with an almighty plop,

Making little muddy bubbles in the foggy light
As it awkwardly, gradually sank from sight.

> *Well, King Arthur was a*
> *Wise old king,*
> *But he didn't hear the facts*
> *About everything.*

The lake was murky and the light was dim
And I saw no mystical samite limb

Or anything else that I pretended,
And thus when I turned around and wended

My way back up to King Arthur's shrine,
I had to invent things — tell him some fine

Story of how I plucked up courage and then took
A mighty throw, and with a beautiful, incisive
       look

About it, the sword fell and entered the water
       clean,
And the smoothest arm I had ever seen

Came up and eagerly clutched it through
Into the silky depths of the evening dew

— It had to be a story, you will surely see,
Fit for a symbol of virility.

*But let's come to the
very revealing point of the
whole discreditable episode —*

    *King Arthur was a
    Wise old king
    But he didn't tell the truth
    About everything.*

King Arthur listened while I had my say,
With a gimlet look that gave nothing away,

Then he rose on one elbow and put out one hand
And pretended he could suddenly understand.

And he said: 'Reversing that history,
Yes, exactly the same thing happened to me,

And the way you describe you finally shot it,
That was the way I originally got it:

The arm that came up to grab and take,
Handed it to me out of that lake.'

> *King Arthur was a*
> *Wise old king,*
> *But no, he didn't tell the truth*
> *About everything.*

And you can blame me and you can blame the king
If you've never done any equivalent thing,

If you've never told some fancy history
To make art cover up for reality.

ENGAGEMENTS IN ARMOUR

'For the first time did I engage in armour,
which I found but a dull satisfaction.'
                     Boswell's London Journal

    I think they hardly happen any more.
    But once, the mettle used to go on with
    Such subtle forethought as was a pleasure
    In itself: happy cumbrances, sweet slow
    Anointments to give safety in the joust.

    The tourney was more honourable then!
    Little was quite so quickly gained as now,
    And yes, there were some kinds of gallantries
    Peculiar to the garb. . . .
                           But now, to wear
    (Half-way, or more, through your warrior's career)

    Nothing but naked ease, this disconcerts.
    You feel you need a ritual to mask
    The lack of mystery in the mystery,
    Some few pretences round it all to hide
    The mawkish fundamentals of the war.

    Or else it gets to be a woman's thing.

TOLD BY A MONK

'When the Saracens overran the shrine at Jerusalem the monks of Little Walsingham announced that the spirit of the Blessed Virgin Mary had taken up residence there . . . the resulting flow of pilgrims brought great wealth to the monastery. . . . Early in his reign Henry VIII walked barefoot to Walsingham to pay homage. . . . Later, at the dissolution of the monasteries, the image of Our Lady was taken to Smithfield and burnt there. . . . The Walsingham shrine is again today a flourishing resort of pilgrims.'
Norfolk guide-book.

    Our Blessed Lady who
    Dwelt in the Holy Land
    Rose from her shrine that was
    Soiled by the heathen hand,

    Soared from that martyred place,
    Ransacked Jerusalem,
    And for her dwelling chose
    Our Little Walsingham
                    Ave Maria

    Then every godly soul
    Who would make offering
    Unto the holy name
    To our new shrine did bring

    Alms and ten thousand prayers
    For her sweet charity,
    So that her presence here
    Made us prosperity
                    Deo gratias

One of that long array,
In cruel barefootedness,
Great Henry came this way
To give, pray and confess.

Walking, a pilgrim, with
Hosed and shoon courtiers he
Tore his royal feet on hard
Stones to our monastery
     In nomine Dei

Suppliant and penitent,
Asking her mercy for
All the sin covered by
The majesty he wore,

Henry bowed down his height
Under her image here,
Many an hour bowed down
In holy pain and fear
     Miserere nostri

All who attended him,
On reverential knee
Fell at his ordering,
Prayed there as long as he,

Then when he rose and stood,
Promised with him to bear
To us and Her always
Tributes of gold and prayer
     To help our holy work

Great Henry went; and was
Cursed of our Heavenly King
For the vile mind he showed
In lustful wandering,

And, for the gold he gave,
This way again he came
Bringing for penitence
Edict and sword and flame
Instead of naked souls

He who was holy once,
Festering with vanity
Thrust his royal power into
Filth and carnality,

Pillaged our golden shrine,
Taking the Image there
To burn in heretic
Fire at a Smithfield fair
No better than a Saracen

Great God is just upon
Avarice and lechery:
King Henry died in grief,
Stricken his treasury,

Useless his proud decrees
Who in sin plunged his . . . head,
Heresy earnt him the
Pox on his dying bed
No more than he deserved

Now again in that spot
Glows our new modern shrine,
And pilgrims render their
Gifts to the Form Divine;

In painted village shops
Priests sell on holy days
Pictures and statues and
Rosaries in her praise
> *Who gave us all we have*

Thus has God's wisdom done
Justice on princes' sin,
And his strong love made gold
Where dross had entered in:

Where shop and shrine lay de-
Cayed under godless feet,
Sweet truth and goodness fills
All the teeth of the street.
> *Amen*

PASTORAL

Some pining cows — with unenchanted sniffing —
Browsed the wan grass. Straggles of green wheat lay
Thrown down by ill-conditioned winds near where
A river dragged past, in a surly way.

Between two stony, grubby settlements,
There was a bend in a connecting lane
Providing, helpfully, some pallid verges,
And here the foxhunt met, in spraying rain.

Sound flesh and arteries swelled boldly outwards
Over the confident bones; the usual
Red coats and leather trouserings were sported;
Their little caps were the identical

Hunt gear for anywhere; and each man had
A placid piebald which, as he proudly sat,
Fumed feathery steam from nostrils set in faces
Looking well-pleased to do what they were at.

An indoor lighting, very blue and feeble
 — A sort-of paintwork of the high sky-shell —
Fell on the hounds, brought up in snarling batches
And loving it, so far as one could tell.

Then, at a billowing horn-call from the master,
Each creature fled off, with a huge sultry bound
After a prey let fly for their pursuing
And chased across a grey and powdery ground.

In all these men and women pride was burning
To have this ceremony in such a place:
The air-locked air smelt grand, the beasts were sprightly,
The clothes were filled with arrogance and grace.

The faces, just as furious and paltry
As were their ancestors' before their births,
Joyed at the springy touch of lunar pastures
As had those solid forebears' on the earth's.

If some forebears had dared to be the first ones,
And radioed back, and from a special bag
Took cameras to photograph each other
And set them up a little national flag,

And gave rehearsed extempore impressions
Of how it felt on their historic day,
And walked around collecting bits and pieces
On screens some ninety thousand miles away,

All this was so that natural human measures
Could dance themselves wherever men might be,
With nothing fine or beautiful neglected,
And nowhere closed to oafish liberty.

TRANSFORMATION SCENE

At the end of
a line of
good, elderly squires
came
this last one,
        geared
to the forces of change,
Master of Foxhounds
but also
graduate of Surrey
(honours
in Business Studies)
and a collector of wines
— who one day
called in his
sharpest tenant-farmer
and his best
shepherd from the
slopes of the dale
        and *his*
smartest
sheepdogs, Rover and
Gyp,
        supreme at
heading
the woolly drop-outs off
— and showed them all
a letter and a
newspaper report;
their valley having
suddenly
become measurable

in terms of a
> capacity
of a different sort from
rearing
sheep.
Because where
conurban
corporations thirsted,
the streams of the mountains
might
> give,
and a full
valley might quench,
and besides the need
was
> paramount
and the squire
quite liked
the idea.
Three years gone,
only ten letters from
affronted Hampstead and
one defused
time-bomb in a
biscuit-tin,
> Gyp
and Rover laze on
the café shores
where the boats
are tethered for
sailing
> on
the reservoir,
the shepherd
stands in charge of the
> tea-urn
or dowses the plastic

cups, the farmer
papers the walls of
the clean new flint
cottage from which
he walks out to
       oversee
the embankments,
and the squire is
addressing a
conference of civil engineers
on 'Landscaping for To-morrow'
at a week-end
       school at
the University of York.
Warm Sundays in summer,
nose-to-tail
in long, loveless
processioning after
what neither
water nor anything
else can provide,
the well-cooled
cars from the conurbation
sidle the new road
to the concreted
edges of the lake,
while back at home
the sprinklers
rotate in solitude
on the lawns of Croft and Mead.

PALINDROME

      We used to be some self-absorbed people living
In a compromised age about twenty years ago. We hated it, it
Was a terrible age, and underneath we liked it in a way, it
      Was because it gave us the chance to feel like that.

      Now it has all changed, and we are older,
And we hate the age completely, not nearly so
Entranced with our hatred. But now there are lots of younger
      People entranced with hatred of this terrible age,

      While underneath they like it in a way, because
It gives them the chance to feel like that. We ourselves feel lost
Because we can't tell them they are compromised like us,
      That being hard for the self-absorbed to see.

      And all the time the ages are getting worse and worse.

WEEPING DOLL

A trapdoor in the pink tin knickers
Of the weeping tin doll set down outside
This chemist's in Notting Hill is
Padlocked, tight, in a little bronze clench.

Open it wide when the key is fetched, and all
Your donations will tumble out, every coin
That activated her high slight wail for
The mortal disease she tells of in

This pitying locality, when you dropped them
Through the slot in her downturned lips.
One need not name the incurable demon (a
Crutch carries one unwithered shoulder

Of this articulate creature) but better celebrate
The goodness of the people spending coins
To make her weep and help her, so she
Lives a little longer on their small change.

Twice a month, a man drives round W.11
To all the dolls, stops his painted van
('The National Society for . . . ') and
Unlocks all the knicker-trapdoors and takes away

Pennies and even sixpences to prop
Her twisting bones. This man has children, too,
Works for them as an accountant for a big company,
And does this voluntarily at night

— It keeps the whole thing personal, and he
Is rather proud of fifteen pounds twelve shillings
Taken from seven dolls in just one trip.
                          A sunlight
No pestering State could hope to intercept

Shines sometimes on this area, where,
Who knows, the very same company may even
Own some of the houses where people try to live
— Enjoying the freedom of their choice to help

Others, and save taxation, and show a lovely
Unforced charity passing by and feeding
The weeping doll with enough stray pennies
To set her wailing many many times a day.

ODE TO CENTRE POINT

        One of the most
Paradoxical of infertil
        -ity symbols
Lately contrived, a vast
        Barren phallus of
Egg-boxes without eggs, it
        Simultaneously wav
-ers and maintains its own
        Projection into the
Soft depths of the sky, a
        Thing of monumental
Insignificance, making no
        Impression and
Quite ignorable, unless for
        Its huge vac
-uity. But in so rapidly
        Appearing, it rased out
Everything lively on its site:
        Small blocks of
Usefully inhabited mansion
        Flats, various
Helpful shops, a passable
        Ristorante, an
Experimental theatre, and
        All of the navigable
Pavement on one side of the
        Charing Cross Road,
Substituting, at ground level, a
        Blue pond inside
Crass concrete walls with square
        -Fingered fountains jetting
The water; and above, shooting upward

          A weird, implacable
Cliff of patterned stone, glass and
          Air, a hive of empty
Cells, tilting, apparently, as the
          Clouds above pass over,
And at one dizzying, approximate
          Count, thirty-three stories high.
Therefore, it impinges on us all,
          Notwithstanding, and needs
To be taken into account; which
          Is why strong men with de
-termination and research have
          Gone grey trying to
Discover why it is there
          (But then who, exactly,
Wanted and actually willed Shell
          Mex or the Euston Road?)
— And what it is to do? Such
          A thing is like the
Clothes without the Emperor,
          Flaunting what looks like
Purpose in order to cover weakness
          And chaos, proving again
That somehow, in our time, all
          Towers are peculiarly
Bad, contraptions of anti-sense,
          Contraceptions of truth,
And things which one day might,
          With the clarity of simply
Looking at what is there, be just taken
          Down and scrapped. Indeed,
What couldn't we do when even
          The few square yards on
Which we base giant follies were
          Fruitful and even
Innocent again, with perfectly
          Natural weeds? To

Have *this* one as a play-space for
    Technocrats to
Run around and play utterly
    Virginal games of Bank Robbers on,
Instead of the real thing,
    Might be a splendid
Idea for its owner to instal
    If he ever repented
Of the tremendous non-use to which
    He put one quarter
-acre of our possible grass. And
    Perhaps one damn good
Roundabout with small, wry,
    Cynical horses' faces to
Ride on, going perpetually grinning
    Round and round would be,
Though futile, a bit more sense.
                      Mean
    -while, until the world
Turns thus inconceivably pure
    And benevolent, the whole thing
Will rear up in front of the eye,
    Narrowing into the heavens and
Widening at its base like some
    -thing unnatural and
Unmotivated found one morning
    In any man's life, and
Probably the result of some
    Nasty and unremembered
Dream.
    Well, in a way, I'd hate
— With its uniformed toughs, trained
Alsatians and all, to knock it down
    And spoil anyone's happy
Fantasies, an act for which I may
    Have no moral right after
So much indulgence of my own,

        But . . . one's most citizenly
Sort of impatience sometimes rises,
      Just as suddenly, wishing
It lugged with it some uncitizenly
        Substance which might go
Off, and reasoning: Reality ought to be
      -gin somewhere, so why not
With somebody else, who has thirty-two
        Stories less of it than me?

FRATERETTO CALLING

for Frederick Grubb

Their glasses are decimalled with dead froth from Europe.
They stubbed the last cigar an hour ago.
Three of this four in the hotel lounge at twelve
Will sleep all night. As they rise, one is saying
'I heard of a Benelux company which . . . .'
         — They are anglers in Lake Erie.

The fourth waits in the whining lift as the
Red circle jumps one by one to the fifth spot.
Gideon's text by the crusted bell-push paint suggests
Write to Amanda c/o 'Personnel'. The Avenger
Ploughs Rosemary through the wet street below as he
         takes some paper from the rack
     So as to angle in Lake Erie.

Amanda has driven the children to System Reading
In the system building, where they push meek buttons
         and watch.
His letter to her is on her formica desk at Tabula
Who have banked the data on this (and on the genes of
A fat dog harrying the bones in the Car Park bin)
         — She is angling in Lake Erie.

Her elder daughter is Diann, Third Girl with Rosemary,
         than whom
She is smarter by as much as 'Minivol' and a Beta
Query Plus in Communications Media. She is ironing
Her caftan under the carpet of the nineteenth boom
         that
Day; and waiting for Pete from I.C.
         To go angling in Lake Erie.

The directors wake and leave, Amanda opens his letter,
Diann replaces the iron, Pete arrives with his guitar,
The dog quits the bones — and they are all separate
Wandering blips killing plankton in a Light Show
           for the Governor
Who is fixing a convenient date for the next revolt:
               With a punched card he opens the sluices
                       which fill the lake.

A POLITICIAN

Today I marshal the sub-divisions of fact.
The statistics
Are marching in various columns
To open the pass.

Tomorrow my equals will fall back out of grace,
Or in failure, or in timely deaths,
And the thunder will be of unmenacing air split by
The applause of the small and less.

And one day, soon after that,
The strategy and the compromise
Will fall away down to my feet like shed grey
                              clothes
That I shall not need to wear.

And I shall be naked again
I shall be
Naked again,
As at the very start.

Then,
The lever will rise to my hand
And the pleasure I take
Will blot out every

Thing
Except
My self,
My truth, my truth.

CLERK

Is a lady of twenty-nine in a
Green, neat tailor-made two-piece, a
White collar, tortoiseshell spectacles and
A smooth skin nourished with the pallor of the Court.

There is a cool one, you say, and are right:
It's in the swift, sleek balance of the wrists
Over the documents, and the voice
(Of the deputy senior prefect of
Her public school) that whispers all day so
Accurate a continual
Transcript of proceedings into
A small white mike.

One dull Tuesday, the sort of day that
Can hardly lift its head to speak its name,
I saw her; from the public seats, thank god.
As usual, the sick with power were busy
Afflicting the sad with none, and she
Was in on this, as she would have to be.

I thought she had a stare might disinfect
Whole seas of toxins.

Part of the time she read the charges out.
Part of the time she jotted little notes.
Her fountain pen was a Parker Duofold.

LEO

A soured mellowness creeps into the light
After the start of July; because
The best of summer is just about now
Worked through, and the evenings seem resigned
To the season having already lost out.
These short fierce stalks are all
That's left in the shorn fields, with someone's
        hay harvest
Reeking off towards the barns. And my
Birthday comes around the middle of all this,

Arriving just past the place when
The marvels assumed of midsummer are dreamt of
As having lain, somewhere untraceable, back,
A little way back, under wet June days; being
There if one only could really have known.
My birthday is therefore a case of thinking
What was it that could have been worth it, if it
Had not unnoticeably gone? The day itself
Inserts a chill under the August sweat,

Especially towards nightfall, especially towards
This time of life; and stands to summer
As the next circle out stands to the bull on
A target: each approximate hit is challenging
Me back to try for summer again. So that
I feel death's final supervening might come
Like a hand holding back the arm which draws,
Still hopefully, the bow; while my voice, thin, and
        just not
Natural any more, is screaming – 'Look, I've only
        just *begun!*'

SYNOPSIS

Two men of forty, who had been to a grammar school, a place suspended between pretension and resignation and unable to opt for either with easy conscience, which had settled both for striving and (to hedge its bets) for admitting that striving was a patent vanity, were climbing Moel Hebog in Snowdonia. At school they had been in the same house, a one-sixth fraction of an institution which divided its four hundred and fifty boys in mystified and apathetic attachment to the names of six Great Victorian literary men. The slope of the mountain was harder than it looked from below, and they went on less out of pleasure than to avert the mockery of friends when they came down. One man, getting stuck on a steep patch of slippery grass, had to be helped up by the other handing down his tie, which he had bought in King's Road, Chelsea, S.W.3.; for they climbed in style and not with expertise. Not far from the ridge that appeared to their friends below to be the summit but was in fact only the first of several successive ridges, they were so exhausted that they decided to make it their objective and pretend they had reached the top. It seemed to them only a small dishonour, because it was so detectable, like walking all of the compulsory cross-country run except for the first hundred yards out of sight and the last hundred yards back. No doubt the simile from school evoked another suggestion, which was not serious: that they write the name of their joint house on a rock and tell their friends, who had been at the same school but in other houses, that they had done so. On the last unbearable feet to their apparent summit, all they had been able, in the true spirit of the school, to settle for, they kept up a joking scrutiny of the idea. To examine motives, to hesitate infinitely in this way, was another characteristic of their education. 'It would show our contempt for the house-system', said one, 'and how little serious effect on us the whole charade had'. 'On the contrary', said the other, 'it would show our respect for it. That is what my psychiatrist would say. It would show just how strong the influence of it was.' 'Perhaps if we were with quite other people; and *then* wrote the name of the house on a rock, *that* would show its influence', rejoined the first, 'but with just us two together, with our "common background of shared trials and shared humour", it becomes a joke'. The second man thought. 'Yes, perhaps, 'he said, 'and yet the fact that we are together, two old members of the same house, climbing this bloody mountain at the age of forty, shows that the influence of the old house was pretty drastic.' And so it continued, with no victory for either point of view. And when they reached their intended first ridge, the first of several visible to them above, but the only one visible to their friends below, now too exhausted even to argue, able only to submit to the lurking strengths of their upbringing, one of them found a small stone soft enough for the other to write the name of the house on a large hard rock. Then they both laughed, equivocal to the end. In such a way, fittingly perhaps in the year which saw the one hundred and forty-seventh anniversary of his birth, was Coventry Patmore celebrated with a graffito on Moel Hebog. And the old house was ambiguously, but definitely, honoured. As was characteristic of the school and its products, the two men had capped a modest and compromised achievement in life with a futile gesture; and they felt they could descend from the point which they had reached. Would it happen like this for the rest of their lives in some squalidly predetermined way?

     Now read on.

NOTES ON SOME OF THE POEMS

Projection. The optical phenomenon described here occurs when car headlights are shone onto the sea — or perhaps other reflecting surfaces — at a certain distance in darkness. When it happened it was altogether accidental; and I have never managed to get quite the same thing since, even in the same place: actually Brancaster Bay, in North Norfolk, so not 'the Atlantic'.

Sadly on Barstools. Michael Miles, the television quizmaster, died in 1971.

Formosavej: is, or perhaps was, a tram terminus in Copenhagen.

Crabwise. The quatrains are versified from an encyclopaedia entry on crabs.

Calypso for Sir Bedivere. It always seems to me that (in Tennyson, at any rate) King Arthur, by telling Bedivere about the 'samite arm', told him exactly what to relate when he came back. In this retelling, I have assumed that he did not tell him beforehand; perhaps did not have anything to tell him. The point is the one about art covering up for life.

Engagements in Armour. The fact that armour in the military, metallic sense was not in use in James Boswell's time has confused some people. The poem is more for those who fortuitously know the context; and not even they are expected to agree with it.

Pastoral. Not long after this was written — I couldn't help feeling it justified the whole fantasy — the first golf ball to be struck on the surface of the moon was putted by one of the members of the crew of Apollo 14.

Transformation Scene. The anti-pollution campaign will not succeed because we have all agreed, or been forced to agree, to use the same terms for utterly different things. Farmers, industrialists and conservationists tend now to come together under the umbrella of the same terminology and persuade themselves that they have a real identity of interest — perhaps it's correcter to say that the first two, plus government and press, are persuading the third. Meanwhile, pollution and spoliation goes on unchecked behind a front of hypocritical concern; the latest public relations stunt for the latest thing.

Palindrome. Really about changing life-styles of radicalism, the difficulty of seeing that the same thing in different clothes is *still* the same thing.

Weeping Doll. Some of the plastic dogs, cats, etc., which collect coins for charity outside shops make a sound — a bell may ring, for example — when money is dropped in. The poem supposes a model of a child which emits a crying sound.

Ode to Centre Point. Centre Point, as everyone now knows, stands, still unoccupied (at time of writing), at the junction of Charing Cross Road and New Oxford Street, London. It has been there since 1963, and it is a tribute to its sheer lack of architectural note and ruthless anonymity that the questions it raises were clear to very few until recently.

Frateretto Calling. If you took the same eighteen hours in the lives of several people closely connected with one another you might get this kind of pattern of interlacing stories. Here it is set in a not-too-far-off future where the technology and the 'governor's' control of the situation (the note of *Transformation Scene* makes the same kind of point about the control of responses) are a little more advanced. The title is from *King Lear* and Lake Erie — there is no life of any kind in it because of man's pollution — seemed a good modern 'lake of darkness'.